Rose and Dad

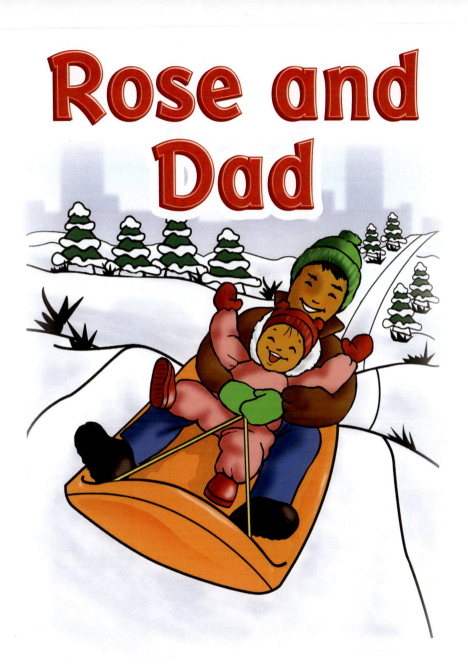

Suzanne I. Barchers

Consultants

Robert C. Calfee, Ph.D.
Stanford University

P. David Pearson, Ph.D.
University of California, Berkeley

Publishing Credits

Dona Herweck Rice, *Editor-in-Chief*
Lee Aucoin, *Creative Director*
Sharon Coan, M.S.Ed., *Project Manager*
Jamey Acosta, *Editor*
Robin Erickson, *Designer*
Cathie Lowmiller, *Illustrator*
Robin Demougeot, *Associate Art Director*
Heather Marr, *Copy Editor*
Rachelle Cracchiolo, M.S.Ed., *Publisher*

Teacher Created Materials

5301 Oceanus Drive
Huntington Beach, CA 92649-1030
http://www.tcmpub.com
ISBN 978-1-4333-2912-8
© 2012 Teacher Created Materials, Inc.

Mom said, "I have to go to the store. Can you cope with Rose some more?"

Dad made Rose a tote.

Then they wrote lots
of notes.

Dad told lots of jokes.

Then Dad tied a lace
that Rose broke.

Dad pulled the sled
with a rope.

Then Dad and Rose
rode down the slope.

Rose slid down a pole.

Then Rose dove in a hole.

Dad and Rose got
cones.

Then Dad and Rose
went home.

Mom got home from
the store. Rose said,
"More!"

Decodable Words

and	got	Mom	slid
broke	hole	more	slope
can	home	notes	store
cones	in	pole	tied
cope	jokes	rode	told
Dad	lace	rope	tote
dove	lots	Rose	went
go	made	sled	

Sight Words

a	that
down	the
from	then
have	they
I	to
of	with
pulled	you
said	
some	

Challenge Words

knock

wrote

Extension Activities

Discussion Questions

- What did Dad and Rose do first? (*Dad made a tote for Rose.*)
- What did Dad and Rose do last before going home? (*They had ice cream cones.*)
- How do you think Dad feels at the end of the story? Why?
- How do you think Rose feels at the end of the story? Why?

Exploring the Story

- Talk about the words *hole*, *home*, and *pole*. Write them so you can see how they are spelled. Discuss how the letter *o* has the long sound as heard at the beginning of the word *old*. Notice that all the words have a silent *e* at the end. Find other words in the story with the same pattern (*cope*, *dove*, *more*, *rode*, *rope*, *Rose*, and *tote*). Then, find other words in the story with the same pattern plus the letter *s* at the end (*cones*, *jokes*, and *notes*). Find other words in the story that have the same pattern but begin with a blend of two consonants (*broke*, *slope*, and *store*).

- Make ice cream pictures by mixing equal parts shaving cream and school glue. Add food coloring to match your favorite flavor or leave it white for vanilla. Drop a scoop on construction paper. Draw a triangle for the cone, or cut a triangle out of construction paper and glue it in place. Allow the creation to dry. The ice-cream paint will stay puffy.